D1608709

New England Decoys

New England Carvers

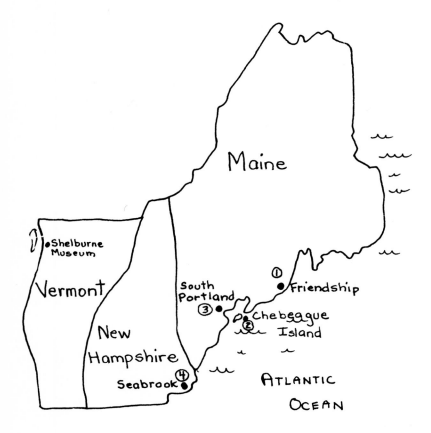

1. George Huey
2. Willie Ross
3. Gus Wilson
4. George Boyd
5. Joseph Lincoln
6. A. Elmer Crowell
7. H. Keyes Chadwick
8. Albert Laing
9. Benjamin Holmes
10. Charles "Shang" Wheeler

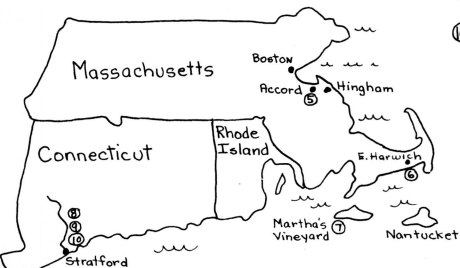

(Not Drawn To Scale)

New England Decoys

by

Shirley and John Delph

Schiffer Publishing Ltd

Box E, Exton, Pennsylvania 19341

Paste-Up: Steve Carothers

Library of Congress catalog card number: 81-51445

ISBN: 0-916838-54-4

Printed in the United States of America

Dedication

To our parents -
*   who taught us that anything is possible if you want it badly enough and are willing to work hard to achieve your goal. Thanks for your love, support, and encouragement!*

Acknowledgements

Ned Covington, Robert Creighton, Dukes County Historical Society, Robert Dwyer, Owen Earnshaw, Gene Gissin, Gary Guyette, Alan Haid, William Howard, Randy Julius, William LaPointe, Philip Lillibridge, Jay Miles, Steve Miller, John Mulak, Ben Pearson, Robert Rich, Bernd Rose, Frank Schmidt, Donald Scothorne, Shelburne Museum, Phyllis Tavares, George Thompson, Joe Tonelli, Steve Tyng, Anthony Waring, Tom Winstel.

Table of Contents

Joseph Lincoln Brant

Introduction

Have you ever tried to put two pairs of hunting pants on over your long underwear at 3 A.M. when your eyes won't open and your zippers won't close? Oh, the joys of hunting! Gathering the necessary paraphanalia: gun, shells, gloves, ad infinitum, I stumbled out the door into a howling snowstorm. This was my last chance to bag a goose and the weather was perfect for goose hunting, if nothing else. Eternal optomist, I continued the 50 miles to Chatham, on Cape Cod. Much to my delight, it stopped snowing in Chatham.

John Mulak and I put out the sneak boats where geese had been feeding regularly. When 40 - 50 geese were spooked off by our arrival, we figured it was our lucky day. We covered our bodies and our boats with white camouflage and waded through the water, breaking ice as we went. Out went John's rig of 35 decoys and we lay down in the boat and waited while freezing rain pelted our faces. Dozens of brant landed (oh, for a brant season) but not a goose in sight. Finally, before terminal numbness set in, a flock of geese circled, left but returned to our call. Visions of juicy roast goose vanished when they took a good look at the two turkeys on the ground and veered away. As the brant continued to splash among the goose decoys, our conversation turned to decoys.

We each ranked the top ten New England carvers and our lists were surprisingly the same. At the top were Elmer Crowell and Joseph Lincoln. These two generate the most interest and bring top prices when they come on the market. Shirley and I decided the book's primary emphasis should be on their birds.

We've included other top carvers, some we're sure would come first on someone else's list, so we plead author's prejudice. Decoys by "Shang" Wheeler, Gus Wilson, George Boyd, Albert Laing, Ben Holmes, and Keyes Chadwick are featured, plus some great unknowns. Although examples of decoratives and miniatures are included, working decoys are stressed. Few decoys from Rhode Island, Vermont, and New Hampshire are found because good examples are seldom found for reasons explained in the chapters.

Without the help of many other people, this type of book is impossible to write, so thanks to all who allowed their collections to be included. A special thanks to these three people: John Mulak and Alan Haid, who went to so much trouble arranging photographic sessions and sharing their knowledge. Randy Julius, twice winner of the Massachusetts Duck Stamp Competition, for taking such beautiful photographs and for the original art work made especially for the book. They're terrific!

Incidently, all I had to show for my hunting trip was a black duck and some good conversation. Talking about decoys is never a waste.

Writing a book like this is a series of compromises between author and publisher — and more complicated than we ever imagined. The cost of printing color pages is mind-boggling, so they must be grouped in 8 page signatures. In order to get in as many color photographs as possible, we had to sacrifice their order of appearance. We hope the index will help you find a specific decoy, but felt the more color the better.

Chapter 1

Hunting In New England

Though these practices of another era are now outlawed-night shooting, baiting with corn, using live decoys, shooting ducks on the water, market gunning, and shorebird hunting-they were once New England traditions. The seemingly endless supply of ducks, geese, and shorebirds that filled the skies and waters encouraged hunters who killed for food, for money, and for sport to kill in quantity.

Hunters generally are hardy individuals, braving poor weather conditions when any intelligent person would stay home. New England offers special challenges of rough seas and cold, bitter wind off the Atlantic Ocean. A winter snowstorm adds additional excitement. Sea duck hunting was especially dangerous. They either went out in boats or waded out into the ocean, fighting the wind and waves for ducks that didn't even taste very good. Winter hunting definitely tested a hunter's dedication. Only the most avid lasted in the brutal weather for long.

Market gunners in the Northeast, as in other parts of the country, slaughtered tens of thousands of birds with no thought of conservation or extinction. The introduction of large bore guns enabled hunters to kill scores with one shot. Restaurants clamored for fresh waterfowl, so demand for their product was high. Many carvers were themselves market gunners at some time in their life; the decoys part of their hunting equipment.

The high prices at market encouraged many questionable customs such as baiting the ponds, bays, and fields with corn. This brought the birds in to feed, where they were sometimes shot on the water at night. Not exactly sporting, but legal until 1913.

Many hunters and gunning clubs kept live ducks and geese year round. Old-timers feel nostalgic, swearing you haven't really hunted unless you've used live birds. The thrill of sitting in the blind, hearing the loud calls and honking, watching the wild birds circling closer and closer until they're within shooting range, cannot be duplicated today. Gunners took advantage of the lifelong mating instinct of geese. One half of the couple had clipped wings and was tethered with a leather strap on the beach or in the water, while the mate was allowed to fly free, joining the migrating flock. Responding to their mate's call, they'd rejoin the tame decoys on shore, luring the wild birds down to the hunters. There they met a barrage of gunfire, never knowing what hit them.

Gunning clubs were popular and ranged from modest to lavish. The Accord Gunning Club was typical with its main

This rig of wooden decoys is strategically placed to simulate the position of live ducks. The wind direction dictates the ideal placement. The greater number of decoys are usually placed downwind in front of a blind. We believe several of the geese decoys are Lincolns.

room for card playing, reading, and boasting, kitchen, and bedrooms. There were pens for the live decoys and a shed for the wooden ones in the back. The blind was camouflaged with ground cover and located near the edge of the pond. The clubhouse's congenial atmosphere was welcome after a long day in the blind.

Wealthy gunners, especially in Rhode Island and Massachusetts, enjoyed all the comforts of home. Some even had tunnels from the lodge to the blind and heaters to keep them warm. All had hunting guides to care for their needs and their guns, helping them to set out the decoys and retrieve the birds. Somehow, without the physical hardship the ordinary hunter endured, the satisfaction of the shoot must have been lessened.

Shorebird hunting was great sport because so many could be slaughtered with one shot. Commonly called "snipe", the shorebirds decoyed easily with wooden and tin stools and whistles. Tin whistles and birds ("tinnies") for each species were sold commercially and were very effective. "Tinnies" were light and could be dismantled, put back in their box, and carried home. Large groups of shorebirds in tight formation were decoyed and one pull of the trigger could fell seventy-five to one hundred, sometimes more. Market hunters filled barrels by the hundreds so they could be shipped all over the country. Spring shooting was a cure for boredom and good target practice as well. Luckily, this insane massacre was banned completely in 1928, although the 1918 Migratory Bird Treaty prohibited the sale of shorebirds commercially.

Times and hunting have changed drastically since the days of the market gunner and the gentleman sportsmen. Hunting is more sporting, more a true test of skill. Conservation of waterfowl and its habitat concerns today's gunner. Some traditions are best replaced with the new.

An original carved silhouette by an unknown maker. It was used as a trade sign. (Collection of John Mulak).

It's a wonder this motley crew didn't scare off every bird in sight! Accord Mass. circa 1910.

It wasn't all hard work, that's for sure! Notice sign that says Birds-In. It was put out when ducks or geese were in the area of the club.

A private hunting club in Accord, Mass., where Joseph Lincoln was once a member. Picture taken in 1945.

All the comforts of home after the hunt. With a kitchen, bedroom, and living room, they certainly wouldn't be roughing it. The sign over the gun rack indicates the hunters were always ready. The sign on the floor says "wait for the word Fire." In earlier hunting days club members would wait until the ducks or geese swam into the decoys and they would all shoot at once while the birds were swimming!

Hanging outside the hunting club shown, above, are enough ducks and geese to make any hunter happy.

The blind was camouflaged with local ground cover. The rig of wooden decoys is seen on the lake, luring unsuspecting ducks to the hunter-and maybe the dinner table. Some slat geese are shown in the bottom left corner.

This self-bailing sea scoter was found washed up on the beach in Maine. Self-bailers allowed water to run out, allowing the decoy to ride the waves better.

Live decoys or tollers were used until 1935 when they were outlawed. Clipped wings kept them from escaping from their pens to freedom. Fall is here and the geese look ready for action.

Live geese decoys are tethered on the beach hopefully attracting the attention of flocks flying overhead.

Chapter 2

Maine

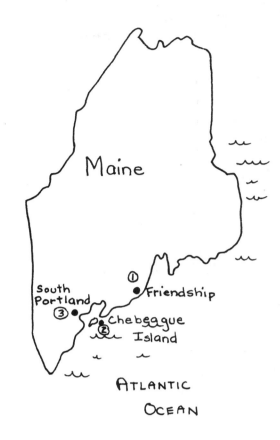

2500 miles of rugged coastline provided Maine hunters and market gunners some of the best hunting imaginable. Enormous flocks of blacks, Canada geese, wood ducks, teal, and goldeneyes passed overhead on their migration south; a large variety of sea ducks and mergansers were also available. Well-rested, well-fed, and unwary, the wild birds were easily decoyed by the tollers riding the waves of the Atlantic.

Blinds dotted the bays along the coast, while more adventuresome hunters took to the open sea to bag surf and white wing scoters, eiders, goldeneyes, and mergansers. The sea duck decoys are generally larger and heavier in order to ride the rolling waves and still be seen. Elaborate painting and carving were secondary considerations, yet many are wonderful sculptural pieces. The effects of rough treatment and salt water often necessitated repainting, so finding scoters and eiders in original paint is unusual.

Interestingly, there are few well-known carvers from Maine, a state which offered large expanses of water and large flocks of waterfowl. There are many magnificent Maine decoys by unknown carvers. Probably made by local hunters to help put some extra meat on the table, their value to a collector is not diminished. "Gus" Wilson, Willie Ross, and George Huey are the most famous carvers from this state, yet little is known of their personal history.

Extremely rare Red-Breasted Merganser hen in original paint and condition. The raised wings, carved eves, and inletted head suggest a Gus Wilson decoy. (Collection of Steve Miller).

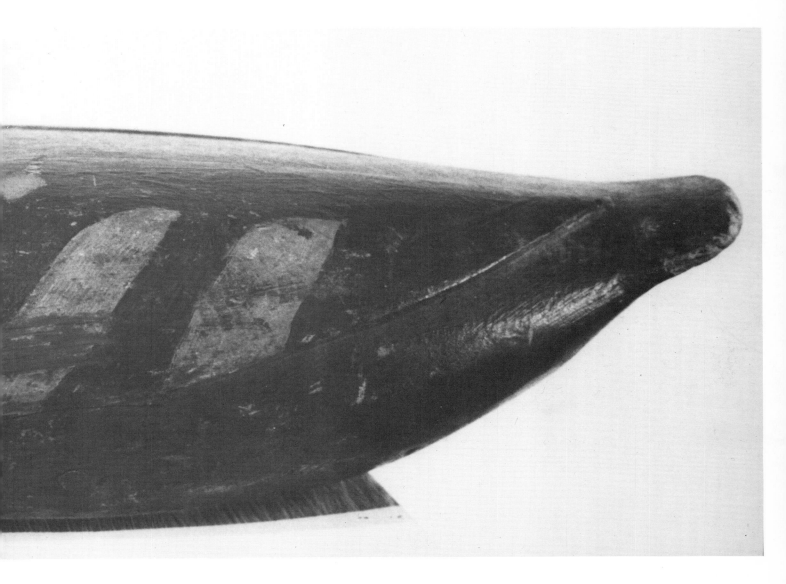

Augustus Aaron "Gus" Wilson (1864-1950). Gus Wilson is known for his sleek, streamlined decoys. While white wing scoters and black ducks are more commonly found, he carved many different species. Wilson did his best carving from 1880 to 1920. The workmanship of his earlier birds is far superior to those he carved later. There was a cruder, more primitive look to them.

Many early decoys were carved at Marshall's Point Light House (near Monhegan Island) prior to 1900, according to Harrison H. Huster's article in *North American Decoys* - Summer 1978. Gus Wilson's rocking head and sleeper decoys were probably made from 1900-1920.

His decoys have flat bottoms, carved eyes, inletted heads, and raised, carved wings. Sleek, simple body lines were sometimes accentuated by intricate bill carving. The open-mouthed merganser with its slit to simulate fish or seaweed is an example. He also carved decoys with mussels in the bill, as did other Maine carvers. The turned-head merganser with a leather crest is a sample of his best carving and painting while the black duck with inletted wings has a decidedly whimsical touch.

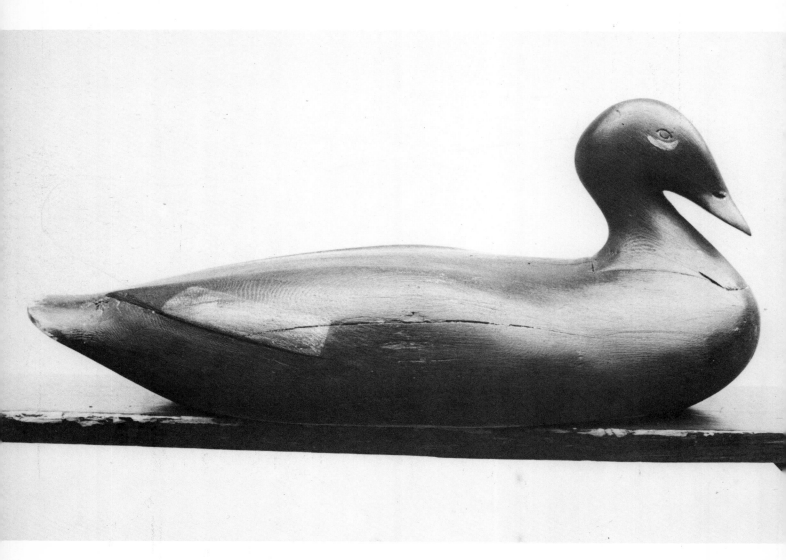

Gus Wilson Rocking Head Black Duck. The head rocked back and forth in rough water, imitating the head motion of the live duck. (Shelburne Museum)

← Stylistic White-Wing Scoter attributed to Gus Wilson. (Private Collection.)

Red-Breasted Merganser drake by Gus Wilson with unusual serated bill. (Quandy Collection).

Red breasted Merganser Drake by Augustus Aaron "Gus" Wilson, South Portland, Maine. Circa 1920. Inletted head. Slit in bill to simulate fish or seaweed. (Collection of Alan G. Haid)

Surf Scoter drake by Augustus Aaron "Gus" Wilson, South Portland, Maine.   Circa 1900.   (Collection Alan G. Haid).

← Gus Wilson Black duck has inletted wings and head. c. 1910. (Collection of Tom Winstel).

"Gus" Wilson White-Wing Scoter with turned head. c. 1900. (Collection of Steve Miller).

Willie Ross Red-Breasted Merganser hen.   (Collection of Joe Tonelli).

Folky Eider from Friendship, Maine area.   (Collection of Gary Guyette).

Shorebird from Ellsworth, Maine with pegs for eyes. (Collection of Gary Guyette).

Oversize Red-Breasted Merganser Drake. Originally had a hair crest. (Collection of Gary Guyette).

Willis Ross lived on Chebeague Island and was a maker of clam baskets. His house and workshop are now in shambles, but his baskets and decoys continue to bring pleasure to collectors. Ross' clam baskets are becoming very valuable which tells you how skillful a basketmaker he was.

He is best known for his beautiful mergansers, though he made black ducks and goldeneyes as well. He carved and painted very simply. A well-carved head, a long body, and an inletted head gave his birds a racy look.

George Huey of Friendship also carved wonderfully sleek decoys. The scoter and merganser drake have the typical Maine inletted head; the stylistic paint on the sheldrake is outstanding. Luckily, no knowledge of his personal history is necessary to appreciate his decoys.

Monheagan Island Preening Scoter.   (Private Collection).

Maine Old Squaw Drake.   (Collection of Donald Scothorne).   →

Maine Eider in worn original paint.   A horseshoe was used as a weight, not too elegant but it does the job.   (Collection of Donald →
Scothorne).

Unknown typical Maine White Wing Scoter.   Old working repaint.
Inletted head.   (Collection of Robert Rich.)   →

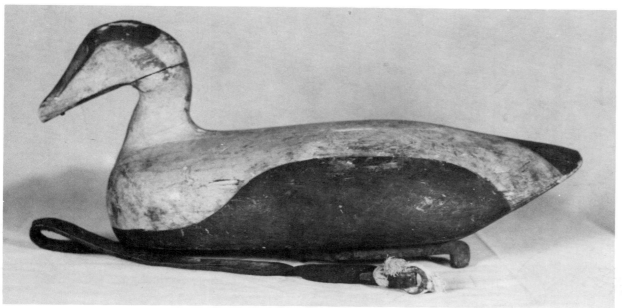

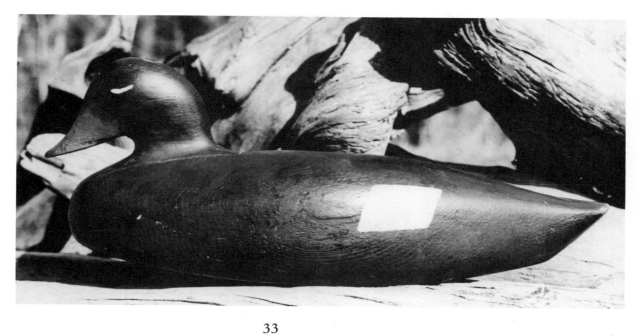

Preening Black Duck by Augustus Aaron "Gus" Wilson, South Portland, Maine. Inletted head. Circa 1905. (Collection of Alan G. Haid.)

Red Breasted Merganser Drake by Augustus Aaron "Gus" Wilson, South Portland, Maine. Circa 1920. Inletted head. Leather Crest. →
(Collection of Alan G. Haid).

Two preening Mergansers by Sam Toothacher of Brunswick, Maine → were made before 1900. (Collection of Phil Lillibridge).

Two of Willie Ross' clam baskets, as sturdy as they are beautiful. Ross made baskets on Chebeague Island, Maine, as well as decoys. →
(Collection of Frank Schmidt).

This exceptionally well carved pair of mergansers represent George Huey's best work. This carver from Friendship, Maine must not have used patterns because his decoys all varied. (From the collection of Jason Miles).

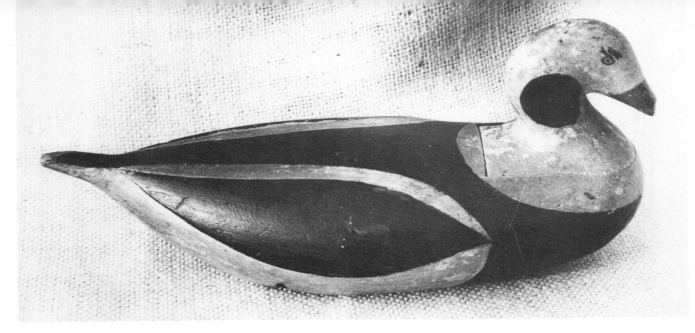

Only 12" in length, this diminutive Old
Squaw is attributed to H. Barry of Maine.
(Quandy Collection).

Maine Eider Hen. Fine Folk art with her
original iron horseshoe weight.
(Collection of Steve Miller).

Preening Monhegan Island Scoter with carved eyes. Inletted neck-separate piece added for head. Crusty old paint showing hard use. (Private Collection).

←   Pair of George Huey Mergansers in original paint typifying his ability to capture the merganser form. (Hen-collection of Frank Schmidt Drake collection of John Delph).

←   Maine Red-Breasted Merganser in original paint and condition. Small portion of horse hair crest remains. (Collection of Phyllis Tarvares).

Red-Breasted Merganser Drake by Maine carver Oscar Bibber. (Collection of Phyllis Tavares).

Exceptional pair of Willie Ross Red-Breasted Mergansers. The very fine paint and unusual bill carving make this pair outstanding. (Collection of Steve Miller).

George Boyd Canada Geese. Canvas covered body and wooden head and breast make for a lighter load. These alert beauties would be →
tempting to geese and geese collectors alike. (Collection of Ben Pearson).

Classic Red-Breasted Merganser Hen attributed to Gus Wilson. Very rare form. (Collection of Steve Miller).

Group of George Boyd miniatures which includes pair of wood ducks, pair of mergansers, pair of buffleheads and swimming goose. (Collection of Owen Earnshaw). →

George Boyd miniature swimming goose. (Collection of Owen Earnshaw.) →

Chapter 3

New Hampshire,
Rhode Island, Vermont

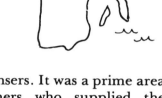

NEW HAMPSHIRE

New Hampshire, with only thirteen miles of coastline, can boast of some of the best wildfowling in New England. The waters of Great Bay and the saltmarshes of Hampton Harbor lured huge flocks of Canada geese, bluebills, goldeneyes, black ducks, and mergansers. It was a prime area for market gunners who supplied the booming Boston market at the turn of the century. Though game was plentiful, excellent hunting skills were a must.

George Boyd trio. Black-Bellied Plovers on either end and Yellowlegs in the center. Easily identified by their beetle-head and distinctive paint style. (Collection of Steve Tyng).

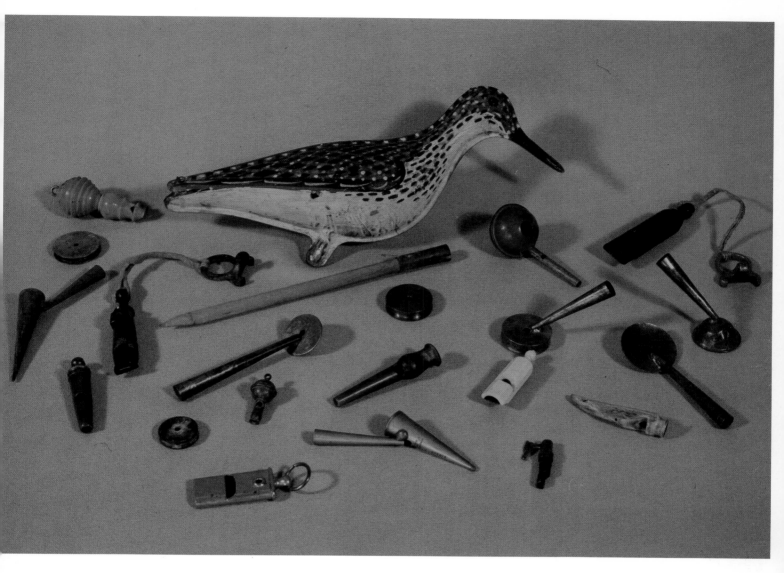

Shorebird Whistles or "Snipe Whistles" as they are sometimes called. Circa 1890-1918. Whistles with holes for two-tone effect are for Plover. Others are for yellowlegs, etc. (Collection of Alan G. Haid).

← Tin Shorebirds by Strater and Sohier, Boston, Mass. Circa 1874. Left to right: Spring plumage Sanderling, Spring Plumage Golden Plover, Spring plumage Sandpiper, Spring plumage Black Bellied Plover. (Collection of Alan G. Haid).

← Shorebirds by Strater and Sohier, Boston, Mass. Circa 1874. Left to right- Ruddy Turnstone, Dowitcher, Robin Snipe and Yellowlegs. (Collection of Alan G. Haid).

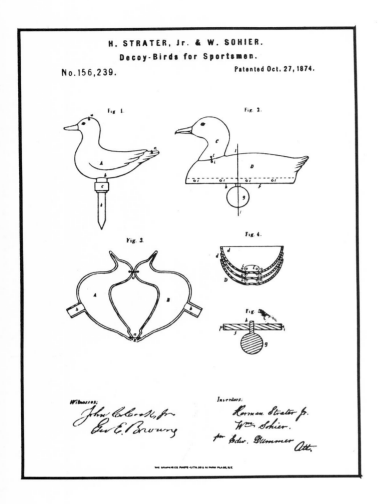

George Boyd (1873-1941) Seabrook, New Hampshire. Market gunning was becoming big business when George Boyd was born in 1873, and it became a part of his life until his early twenties. He worked the Seabrook saltmarshes as hay cutter and market gunner until his marriage brought a career change - to shoemaker in the local factories.

He had a workshop behind his house where he did finishing work on the shoes, and it was here that his early working decoys were made. He mastered wood as well as leather, carving plovers, yellowlegs, Canada geese, mergansers, black ducks, and goldeneyes. Years of hunting and working in the marshes enabled him to create a realistically carved and painted decoy.

Iver Johnson & Company, a fine sporting goods store in Boston, sold his plovers and yellowlegs in the early 1900's. They also carried Elmer Crowell's decoys, so Boyd was in very good company.

Most of his miniatures were made after his retirement in the early 30's, although he did carve some special-order working decoys and a few geese. Boyd continued carving until his death in 1941. George Boyd's miniatures covered a wide variety of species from old squaws to puffins, teal to ruddy ducks, and are evidence of his skill with a palette and paintbrush. Macy's and Abercrombie & Fitch admired them enough to sell them in their New York stores for a whopping 50 cents.

The amazing thing is that the carver of these magnificent decoys and miniatures was unknown until early 1970's when research uncovered the identity of this talented craftsman.

In his folio, *George Boyd The Shorebird Decoy. An American Folk art,* Winthrop Carter discusses the distinctive "squared-off" beetle heads and short brush strokes that make Boyds easily identifiable. Meticulous care was taken with each decoy, sanding, priming to bring out the grain, then sanding again. Old telegraph poles and railroad ties provided the seasoned cedar he needed; his memory was the only pattern he used, making his decoys custom made.

Boyd made canvas-covered geese that are works of art with the typical Boyd head of wood, a wooden breast and tail, and body of canvas-over-wood. A friend of ours remembers his father's rig of solid Boyd geese. At the time, he wasn't to impressed after hauling them around. Too bad they've all been lost or given away.

George Boyd's working shorebirds, with their squarish, "beetle-heads" and short brush strokes, are more common than any other species of working decoys. His output of miniatures is said to be around 700. The masterful carving and painting make his working birds and miniatures extremely collectible for their beauty alone. This Yankee craftsman knew what he was doing!

A gaggle of George Boyd geese. (Collection of Ben Pearson).

George Boyd, Seabrook, New Hampshire, carved these two Black-bellied Plovers. (Collection of Steve Miller.)

RHODE ISLAND AND VERMONT

Despite miles of shoreline, Rhode Island carvers produced few decoys; there isn't a "name" carver in the bunch. Market gunners left the hunting to the rich sportsmen of the era. Lack of marshland made open water hunting necessary and unprofitable. Too many men were needed to set the rigs, cutting into the profits made at the market.

Wealthy Newport hunters mainly used factory and commercial decoys because expense was not even a consideration. Many Mason and Crowell decoys were used on Narragansett Bay. The less affluent hunters probably carved their personal stools, but no Rhode Island commercial carver of significance has surfaced.

Vermont, not surprisingly, produced few decoy carvers, yet the largest and finest decoy collection open to the public is there. The Shelburne Museum's Dorset House is a must for every serious collector.

George H. Bacon, Burlington, Vermont (1861-1925), hunted in the Lake Champlain area and carved several hundred ducks. Well-carved heads and a simple paint and body style make Bacon the premier Vermont carver.

Very delicate Yellowlegs by George Boyd. 100 % original condition with characteristic Boyd beetle head, shoe button eyes, split tail, and uncontrived painting. (Collection of Steve Miller.)

George Boyd Black-bellied Plover
in unused condition. (Quandy collection).

51

The Mason Decoy Factory, Detroit, Michigan. (1894-1924), supplied many New England hunters. White Wing Scoters and Shorebirds were hunted heavily in the Northeast. Shown is a Tack Eye Scoter, a Robin Snipe, and a Yellowlegs. (Collection of the authors).

The Mason Decoy Factory provided many decoys in the New England area like this challenge Grade Black Duck. Gun powder was stored in cans such as this very early on by the Dupont Company. The metal lid is attached to fabric binding tape which encircles the can vertically. A paper label was then glued over the tape. (Collection of John & Shirley Delph).

Rhode Island Goldeneye Hen. (Collection of Bill LaPointe).

Rhode Island Goldeneye Drake. (Collection of Bill LaPointe).

Frank Owens, South Burlington, Vermont Redhead Hen, c. 1831, was carved by Owens, a local stonemason. This solid bodied decoy was used in the Lake Champlain area. (Shelburne Museum).

George H. Bacon, Burlington, Vermont. Made this Blue Bill Hen. Simple lines & paint were Bacon's style. (Shelburne Museum).

Folky Goldeneye Hen, probably from Vermont, has extended paddle tail and well-carved head. (Private Collection).

Factory decoys, like this Dodge Merganser, were often used by New England hunters and hunting lodges. Rather than carve their own, more affluent hunters would order their decoys from sporting goods stores, such as Iver Johnson, and others ordered directly from the factory. Advertisements in various sporting journals enticed prospective buyers with various claims of success. (Private Collection).

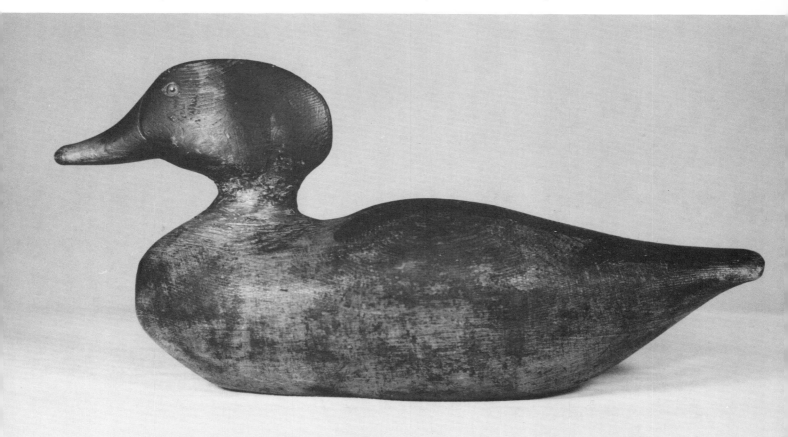

George H. Bacon, Burlington, Vermont, (1861-1925) carved this pair of Goldeneyes. They were used on Lake Champlain, an excellent hunting area.

Bacon decoys are rarely found today although he carved several hundred blocks. (Shelburne Museum).

Chapter 4

Connecticut

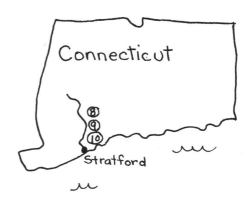

Stratford, Connecticut, was home to three of New England's finest carvers; Laing, Holmes, and Wheeler, founder of the "Stratford School". Located on the Housatonic River, conditions dictated the type of decoy best suited to the area. The waters of Long Island Sound and the Housatonic were calmer than those in Massachusetts and Maine, so a large, heavy decoy was unnecessary. Hunters had other problems - strong currents and slush ice tended to tip over the "rocking horse" decoys used before in 1960's. Albert Laing created a decoy whose style and function met these challenges, becoming the prototype for countless others.

"Stratford" birds have several features which make them easily identifiable: a rounded tail, a groove behind the head, and a prominent, extended breast. While there is an obvious similarity to their decoys, each put his stamp of individuality on his birds.

Albert Davids Laing, father of the "Stratford School", was the son of a wealthy New York textile manufacturer. An avid "gentleman" hunter, he kept a detailed hunting journal from 1831-1836 and 1863-1886. Laing moved to Stratford during the interim period after a fall-out

with his family. Here he became a gentleman farmer as well.

Laing so disliked the "rocking horse" decoys used in the area, finding them clunky and unwieldy, that he carved his own stools. He felt he could make a decoy aesthetically and functionally superior to those available. His innovative talents resulted in the "Stratford" decoy. The extended breast enabled the ducks to ride over the slush ice and not get tipped over.

Laing used white pine for his hollow bodied decoys and they were weighted with a pear-shaped weight. Some are branded LAING but the majority are not marked. The seam where the body halves were joined was above the waterline and fastened with copper nails, another Laing innovation. Copper nails didn't rust away and split the wood as did the galvanized nails commonly used. The extra expense was minimal but the increased durability was maximal.

Albert Laing carved ducks with various head position, from lowheads to sleepers, yet all his ducks have rounded, paddle tails. Laing's expertise as a carver was one legacy not included in his will, but passed on nevertheless.

Benjamin Holmes (1843-1912) emulated his predecessor's carving style, yet his lifestyle differed greatly from Albert Laing's. As a carpenter and professional decoy maker, he enjoyed a friendship with Laing, but the difference in social status and age made it that of teacher to student.

Under Laing's tutelage, Benjamin Holmes developed great carving and painting skill. In 1876 a dozen blue bills were entered in the International Centennial Exposition in Philadelphia, and Holmes came out the winner!

Like Laing, he used white pine for his hollow bodies but Holmes made a noticable design change. The two body parts were of unequal size. Holmes used a ½ inch bottom borad and a larger top section, with the seam below the waterline. The reason for this difference is supposition but William Mackey felt it was an attempt to assert his independence and give his decoys his personal stamp.

Benjamin Holmes, also like Laing, carved primarily black ducks, bluebills or scaup, and goldeneyes, although they were known to carve a few scoters. Ben Holmes successfully carried on the tradition of carving excellence and fully deserves his acclaim.

Charles E. "Shang" Wheeler, the last member of the famous Stratford trio, is by far the best known. Wheeler's love of the outdoors influenced his life, both his vocation and avocation. As a young man he was a sailor and a market gunner for a time; later he worked at an oyster farm as inspector and manager. His free time was spent hunting along the Atlantic coast. "Shang" carved his first decoys for his personal rig when only a teenager. The "Stratford" style was adopted by Wheeler and refined to perfection.

Public service filled much of his later life when he served as a Connecticut State Senator. Conservation of natural resources was a main concern and he was an effective champion of the cause as a member of the State Game Commission. Carving was for his personal pleasure, never money. He

ended up giving his decoys away to friends.

Like Laing and Holmes before him, Wheeler won acclaim in a decoy carving competition. In 1923 he won the silver cup and the grand championship in the first decoy show held in the United States in Bellport, Long Island, New York.

Many collectors feel Charles E. Wheeler exhibited the most versatile talent and skill of the three. Wheeler made both wooden

Hollow Blue Bill Sleeper by Albert Laing.   (Shelburne Museum).

and cork decoy, including a wide variety of species. His wooden decoys are found in various head positions, deftly carved and painted. Like Laing's, the hollow pine bodies were of equal sizes with the seam above the waterline. His superb paint style is clearly shown on the championship mallard drake. In his later years, Wheeler carved many decorative decoys which are highly prized by collectors today.

Cork decoys were used on calmer waters in the area. The unadorned cork body was accented by a well-carved wooden head and tail. A heavier weight was used to help them ride the water correctly. Anyone who lavished so much effort on a cork decoy must truly have loved to carve! "Shang" Wheeler's love of carving can only be surpassed by a collector's joy of owning one of his magnificent decoys.

Albert Laing Lowhead Whistler Drake & Hen. This pair have the tucked head position of a duck at rest. (Shelburne Museum).

A.Laing Surf Scoter. The extended breast of the Stratford area is not noticeable because of its sleeping position. (Shelburne Museum).

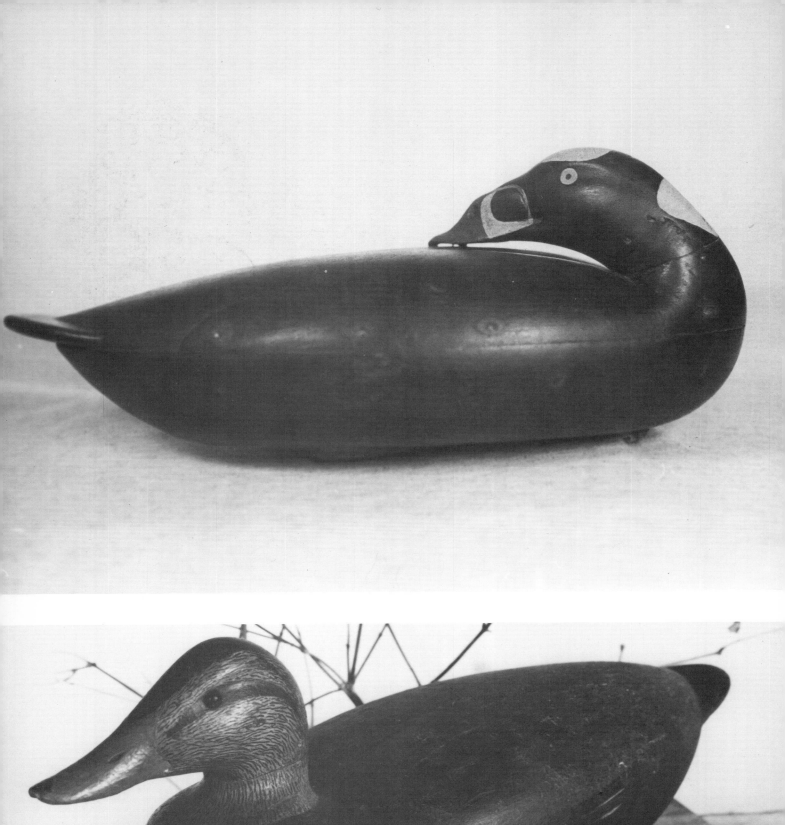
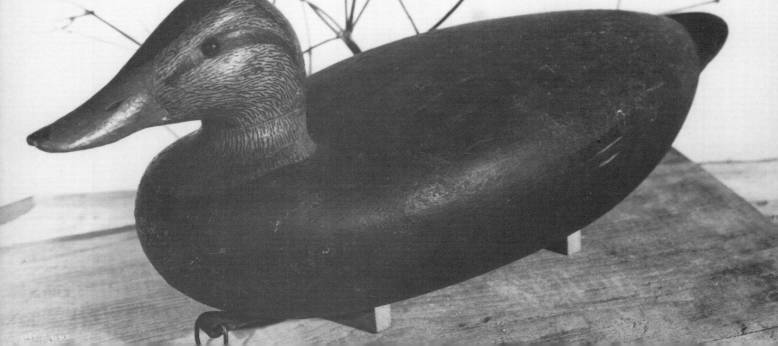

Ben Holmes whistler hen.   Contented position and fine paint.
(Shelburne Museum).

Extremely rare Albert Laing preening surf scoter.   (Collection of
George Thompson).

Albert Laing, predecessor of Benj. Holmes and "Shang" Wheeler,
carved this hollow-bodied Black Duck.   One feature is the joint seam
that floats above the water line.   (Shelburne Museum).

Ben Holmes Whistler Drake. Extended breast and one half inch bottom board. These decoys were used on the Hoosatonic River in Connecticut. (Shelburne Museum).

Somewhat battleworn Ben Holmes Black duck that certainly has been →
"freshened up" many times in its life. (Shelburne Museum).

Ben Holmes Black Duck with characteristic V groove in back and →
½" bottom board. (Shelburne Museum).

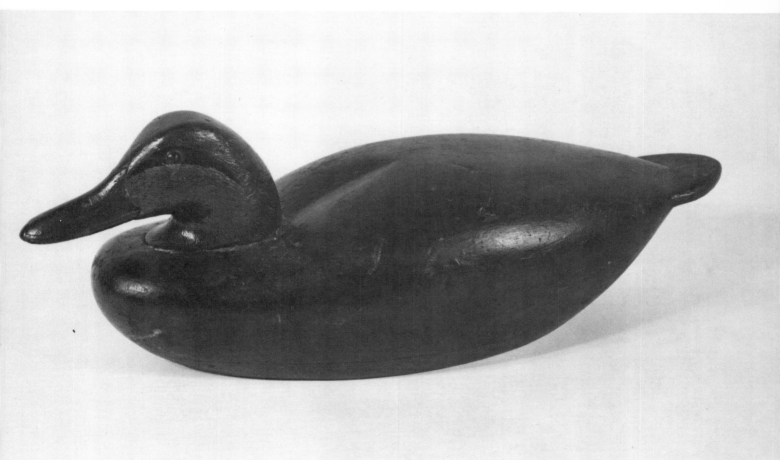

65

Charles E. "Shang" Wheeler entered this Mallard Drake in the first decoy show competition in 1923. He won a silver cup and the grand championship-not a bad start! The well-carved head and body are complimented by exquisite paint. (Shelburne Museum).

Two different views of Shang Wheeler Sleeping black duck. Pristine condition. (Collection of Tony Waring). ↓ →

H.Keyes Chadwick Redheads.   (Private Collection).

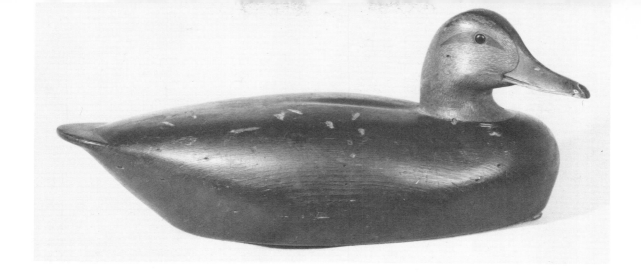

Charles E. "Shang" Wheeler Black Duck. (Collection of Joe Tonelli).

A wonderfully carved Black Duck head attached to a simple cork body. Shang Wheeler made these decoys for use on sheltered water. The weight and Keel are heavier than those on his wooden decoys. (Shelburne Museum).

← "Shang" Wheeler White-Winged Scoter. (1924). Made of balsa, the bill carving is exceptionally well done. (Shelburne Museum).

← Never intended for hunting, this Shang Wheeler Broadbill drake is in mint condition. His later decoys were mostly for ornamental or exhibition use. (Shelburne Museum).

An example of Henry Keyes Chadwick at his best. His carving skill speaks for itself. The Redhead Drake and Hen exemplify Chadwicks simple, yet functional paint style. (Private Collection).

This Widgeon Drake by H.K. Chadwick is evidence that his assumption that he wasn't a talented carver was false. In a letter to a friend in 1949 he states "although my efforts didn't amount to much, as you know, I wasn't a "specialist" so anything else don't count." In a 1947 letter he says, "as I spoil my work with paint. I wouldn't even pass as a housepainter, let alone an artist as is Mr. Crowell. (Dukes County Historical Society).

70

Unknown Hollow Massachusetts red breasted merganser hen. Very early with seperate carved wooden comb. (Collection of To ny Waring).

An unknown carver, probably from Massachusetts, made these American Mergansers. The head carving and paint detail is exceptional. (Collection of Joe To-nelli).

71

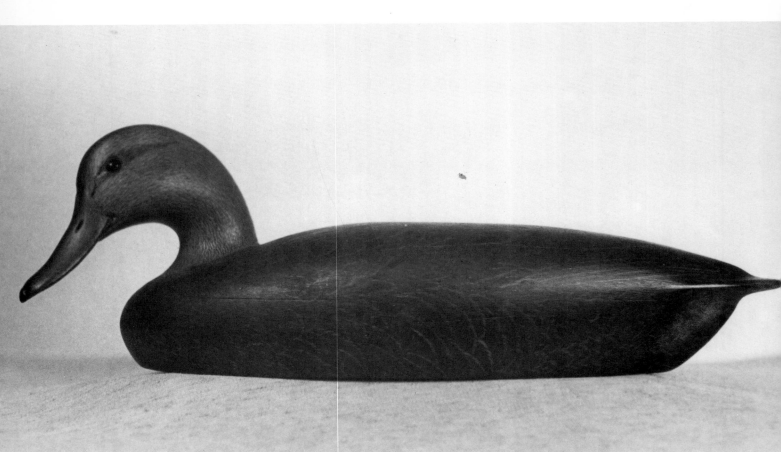

72

Joel Barber (1877-1952) Mallard Drake.   Author of *Wild Fowl Decoys* (1932), Joel Barber qualifies as the original decoy "collector."   He began collecting in 1918, drawn to decoys as sculpture, as an art form. Barber's architectural skills enabled him to draw wonderful watercolors and sketches of decoys and to carve excellent decoys.   He spent years amassing birds from all over the country, and shared his collection with others through exhibitions and decoy shows.   After his death, his beloved collection was presented to the Shelburne Museum in Shelburne, Vermont, so that more people could share in his love affair with "ducks". (Shelburne Museum)

← This Shang Wheeler Sleeper Black Duck was found in the loft over his shop after his death and was acquired from the Wheeler estate by Joel Barber.   (Shelburne Museum).

← "Shang" Wheeler Black Duck.   (Collection of George Thompson).

74

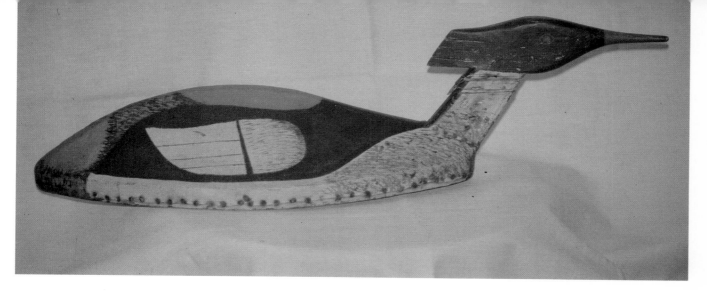

Unique Massachusetts (Cape Cod) Red-Breasted Merganser Drake. It has a flat silhouette head and a canvas-over-wood frame body. (Quandy Collection).

This pair of Ben Smith Canvasbacks represent some of the finest decoys ever found on Marthas Vineyard. (Collection of Dukes County Historical Society).

Martha's Vineyard Red-Breasted Merganser Drake (maker unknown). A solid body decoy made of cedar. The expert carving and paint treatment make you wish you had one on your shelf. (Collection of George Thompson).

Cape Cod Red-Breasted Merganser Drake (maker unknown). The original horse-hair crest gives it a racy look. (Collection of George Thompson).

Massachusetts Black-bellied plover by unknown carver has excellent feather painting, painted eyes, and a wooden bill. (Collection of the authors).

Joel Barber Blue Bill Drake. His book, *Wild Fowl Decoys*, shifted
← emphasis to decoys as collectible art forms. His collection of decoys
and paintings are exhibited in the Dorset House, Shelburne Museum.
(Quandy Collection).

← Canvasback drake by Joel Barber. Solid body and raised carved
tail feathers. (Shelburne Museum).

Roswell E.Bliss, Stratford, Conn., carved this pair of Old Squaws
Drakes. (1887-1967) (Shelburne Museum)

Lothrop Holmes, Kingston, Massachusetts, made the folky canvas-covered Old Squaw. (Private Collection).

Canada Geese by Captain Osgood, Salem, Massachusetts. C. 1849. Hollow bodies and detachable necks made them easier to transport. Included are a preener, a feeder, and 3 with the alert head positions. (Shelburne Museum).

Ready for the hunt! Decoys, gun, gun powder, and shell boxes are items hunters would have needed. The walnut gunning box has brass 10 gauge shotgun shells and loading tools. Smokeless gun powder was poured in the empty cartridge out in the field. The Winchester paper shells were loaded and ready to go.

American Merganser drake by Franklin Pierce Wright of Massachusetts. (Collection of Tony Waring).

RANDY JULIUS

A. Elmer Crowell Mallard Drake

Chapter 5

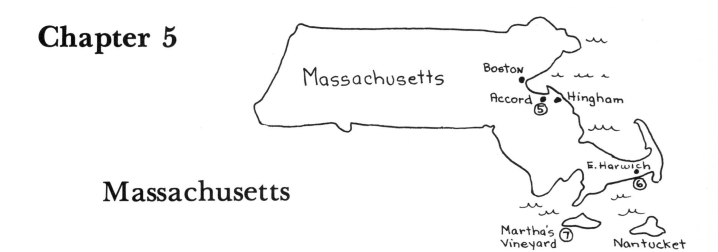

Massachusetts

HENRY KEYES CHADWICK (1865-1958)

Martha's Vineyard, four miles south of Cape Cod, with its ideal wildlife habitat was a hunter's paradise during the late 1800's and early 1900's. Most hunting took place on the salt marshes, bays, and ponds where rigs of bluebills, black ducks, redheads, goldeneyes, mergansers, and shorebirds enticed wild ducks within shooting range. Other species, canvasbacks, mallards, buffleheads, and teal, were carved in lesser numbers. Coming by the thousands, the migratory birds found Martha's Vineyard the perfect stopping-off place on their long flights north and south each year.

Growing up in such a sporting environment, it must have been a natural progression from hunter to carver. Most local hunters lacked the means and the inclination to get "store-bought" decoys, preferring to fashion their own. No doubt thinking theirs looked and worked better anyway.

Henry Keyes Chadwick (1865-1958); Oak Bluffs, Massachusetts, a Vineyard native, is the best known carver from the island, and certainly one of the best. His first decoys were carved for his personal hunting rig in 1881 at the age of 16, though none of these have ever turned up.

Fate seems to have played a part in Chadwick becoming a professional carver. His sole ambition was to raise fancy poultry, but lack of finances forced him to abandon his dream. Instead he became a carpenter and calligrapher. He was almost forty before he was able to raise chickens, yet continuing with his carving and calligraphy.

Keyes Chadwick started carving decoys to sell after an accident temporarily laid him up and he was unable to do carpentry work. His decoy production continued sporadically until 1951, carving 1500-2000 birds in his lifetime.

He was greatly influenced by his contemporary, **Benjamin D. Smith** (1866-1946). A carpenter, neighbor, and market gunner in season, Chadwick used Ben Smith's decoys as his prototype.

Chadwick's decoys are prized for their simplistic style, with no extraneous carving or brush strokes to be found. Admittedly, his expertise with a paint brush was limited, but sculpturally his decoys are magnificent. Intricate, detailed feather painting seems almost out of place, detracting from the smooth lines. When Elmer Crowell's stock was low, he would buy unpainted birds from Keyes and paint them himself. Although masterfully painted by Crowell, the overall impression suffered. Keyes Chadwick was a carver whose decoys looked beautiful without a speck of paint.

He carved solid, flat-bottomed birds with cedar bodies and sugar pine heads. His earliest birds (pre-1920) were more delicately carved and detailed, had slimmer necks, and undercut tails. Unfortunately, they damaged easily so he altered his style. The tails were shortened and rounded, necks were thickened, and some detailing was eliminated, making it a more functinal decoy. A round, poured lead weight, flush with the bottom, is found on birds made after 1900.

Chadwick had a one man assembly line, carving groups of bodies, then groups of heads. While most decoys have good quality glass eyes, some have metal studs or painted eyes. He used straight demarcation lines when painting. Having little confidence in his painting ability, he used cardboard patterns when doing intricate speculums.

In his book, *Martha's Vineyard Decoys,* Stanley Murphy quotes Chadwick in a 1950 interview for the *Vineyard Gazette* as saying, "I've never done what I wanted to do, and that was to raise chickens, just to raise lots of champion chickens." While Keyes Chadwick felt his decoys were of no importance, collectors today would protest strenuously. Henry Keyes Chadwick was a master carver whose decoys are greatly prized acquistitons in any collection.

Unknown Canada Goose from Fern Island Club-Hansen, Mass. Canvas over wire frame. Not a common Massachusetts form. (Collection of Robert Rich).

Pair of "middle" period H.Keyes Chadwick Redheads. (Private Collection).

Humorous Goldeneye Hen?? Very old decoy. Ancient crackled paint. Found on the North River, Marshfield, Mass. (Collection of Robert Rich).

Tiny Goldeneye Drake. Laminated body. Original paint. From Duxbury
Massachusetts. (Collection of Robert Rich).

Unknown Massachusetts shorebird. Yellowlegs?? Painted eyes, original paint.
Very old replaced bill. (Collection of Robert Rich.)

"Loomer" Goose decoy, pine frame construction. "Board" head. From Fern Island Club-Hansen Mass. (Collection Robert Rich.).

Two exceptional Elmer Crowell Canada geese. Superb form and excellent paint. (Decoy on left-collection of Bob Dwyer. Decoy on right-collection of Tom Winstel).

Golden plover. Red-breasted Merganser drake. Circa 1850. Made by an unknown hand. Both pieces reflect a similar style in carving and painting. Decoys
have raised carved wings, round carved eyes and same black and white color
tones. Plover is branded W.S. Morton. Merganser is unmarked and hollowed
out from bottom. (Quandy collection).

Golden Plover, branded W.S. Morton. Mr. Morton was born in 1809 in
Milton Mass. and moved to Quincy, Mass. in 1850 where he did most of his
gunning. He died in 1871. (Quandy Collection).

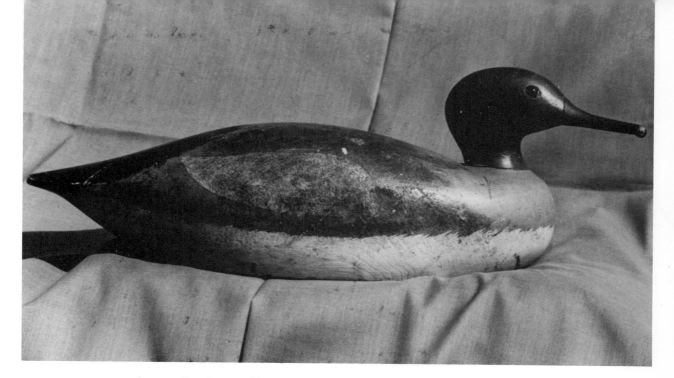

A very fine hen red-breasted merganser by H. Keyes Chadwick. Martha's Vineyard. Mass. Circa 1935. (Quandy Collection).

3 Massachusetts Golden plovers with inletted tails and baleen bills. Tack eyes. Originally had two wire legs in each bird. (Collection of Herbert Schiffer).

Yellowlegs attributed to Joseph Lincoln, very delicate carving. (Collection of Herbert Schiffer).

Golden plover. Mass. c. 1880. (Courtesy Herbert Schiffer Antiques).

Burr family Black-bellied plover. Raised wing carving, dropped tail and superb paint. Hingham, Mass. Circa 1910. (Collection J. Delph).

Canvasback drake by Ben Smith. Hollow and superbly painted. (Collection Dukes County Historical Society).

Canvasback hen by Ben Smith. Mate to drake in previous picture. (Collection Dukes County Historical Society).

Elmer Crowell Canvasback drake with exceptional carving on back. Circa 1900. (Collection Dukes County Historical Society.)

H.Keyes Chadwick Barrows Goldeneye drake. Very rare species. (Collection Dukes County Historical Society).

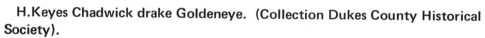

H.Keyes Chadwick drake Goldeneye. (Collection Dukes County Historical Society).

Chadwick Red-breasted Merganser. Battleworn survivor of heavy duty cape
hunting. (Collection of Dukes County Historical Society).

Pair of Vineyard Black ducks. Very racy head style. (Collection of Dukes
County Historical Society.)

Unknown Vineyard Preening Bluebill drake. (Collection of Dukes County Historical Society).

Very rare H.Keyes Chadwick Brant. Only 12 made. (Collection of Dukes County Historical Society).

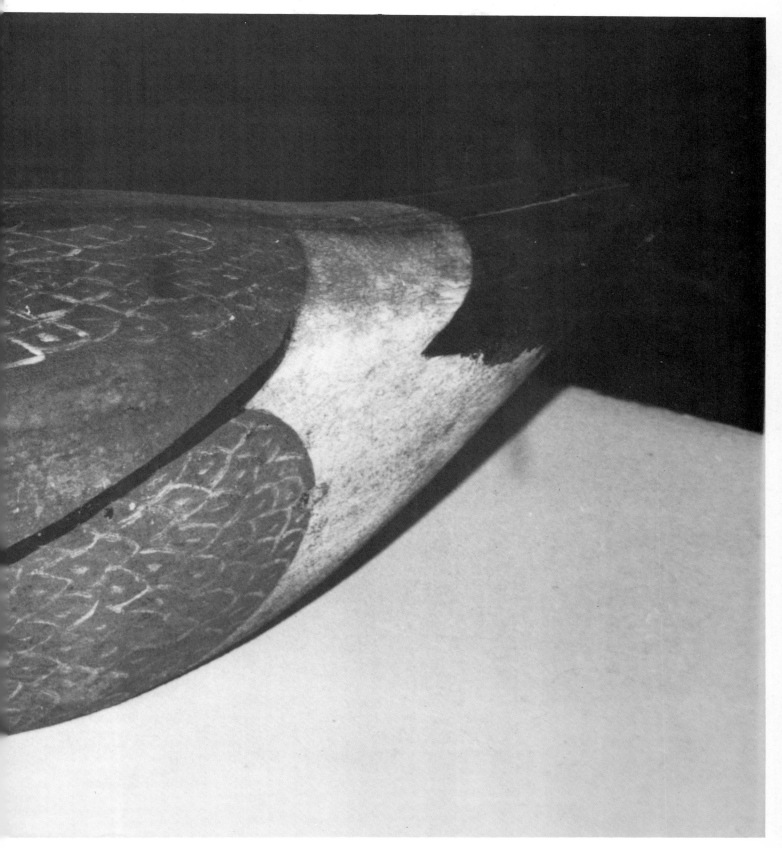

H.Keyes Chadwick Blue Bill drake from Foote rig. (Collection of Tony Waring).

Mint condition Blue Bill hen by H.Keyes Chadwick. (Quandy Collection).

Henry Keyes Chadwick Redhead Drake.

Joseph Lincoln Black Duck with great head style. (Collection of John and Shirley Delph).

A masterpiece by Joseph Lincoln. This Canada Goose with its aggressive head position is called a swimming goose. A hunter wanted geese with various head positions to give his rig a more natural look. (Collection of Phyllis Tavares).

Joe Lincoln canvas covered White-Winged Scoter with a wooden head. (Private Collection).

4 Lincoln Black Duck Heads. While nearly identical in form, there are variations in the bill coloring. (Collection of Tony Waring).

"Lincoln type" Yellowlegs. Beautifully painted and carved, they have glass shoe button eyes, wooden bills, and raised wings. (Private collection.)

Sampling of Joseph Lincoln miniatures (Left to right). Redhead Drake, Blue Bill Hen, Blue Bill Drake, Preening Canada Goose, Mallard Hen, Mallard Drake, American Merganser Drake. Wood Duck Drake in foreground. (Private Collection).

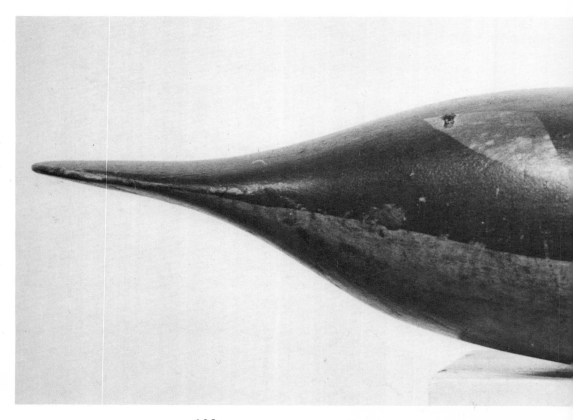

100

Merganser by H. Keyes Chadwick. Traces of original paint on head on this stylishly simple decoy. (Collection of Steve Miller).

Red-breasted Merganser drake with original horse-hair crest and paint. Rockport, Mass. Circa 1890. (Collection of Steve Miller).

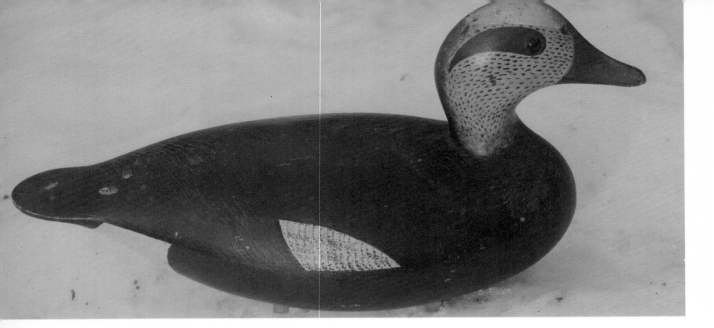

Joseph Lincoln Widgeon Hen. A very rare species; few were made by Lincoln. (Shelburne Museum).

Widgeon Drake by Joe Lincoln. Subtle painting and carving characterize Lincoln's decoys. (Shelburne Museum).

American Brant by Joseph Lincoln exemplies an artful simplicity of paint and form. (Collection of John and Shirley Delph).

Full-sized shore-birds by E.Crowell, which were sold as decoratives. Yellowlegs on left and Hudsonian Curlew on right are in a running position. (Private Collection).

These full-sized decoratives by A.E. Crowell were sold as "mantle" birds. Great care was taken with the carving and painting of the Yellowlegs and Black-bellied Plover. (Private Collection).

Collection of Elmer Crowell miniatures. Left to right. Mallard Drake, Wood Duck Drake, Hooded Merganser, Bufflehead Drake, Red-Breasted Merganser Hen, and Mallard Drake. (Private Collection).

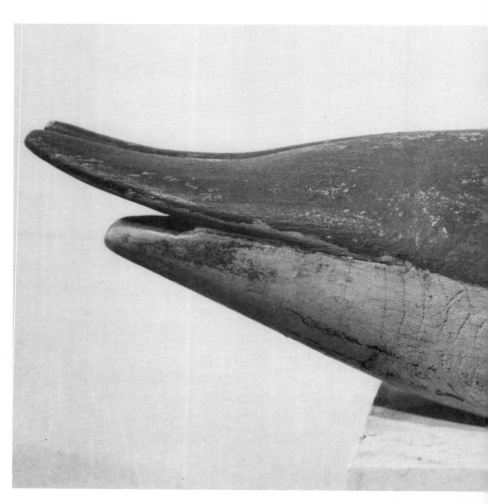

Fine old Massachusetts Merganser found in Chatham, Mass. The hollow construction and head and tail carving make this decoy outstanding. (Quandy collection).

Gull-Confidence decoy attributed to Frank Richardson, Martha's Vineyard tail is pieced into the body. Gulls are rare and this example is exceptional. (Collection of Steve Miller).

Crowell cork Mallard Hen with wooden head and bottom board. (Private Collection).

Another version of a Crowell Black Duck. (Collection of Steve Tyng).

Elmer Crowell Mallard Drake with raised wings. (Pre-stamp) (Collection of Steve Tyng).

Elmer Crowell Mallard Drake.   (Collection of Robert L. Dwyer).

Subtle feather painting on the Elmer Crowell Blue Wing Teal Drake and Hen is evidence of his talent as a painter.   These are quite rare as Crowell seldom carved teal.   Both have carved wing tips and oval brands.   (Private Collection).

4 shadow decoys. The Mergansers, found in Portland, Maine, are from a rig of 12. They have flat bodies and 3 dimensional heads and were nailed onto a frame. Circa 1920. (Collection of Steve Miller).

Rare Widgeon Drake with raised wings and preening head was made as a working decoy by A. Elmer Crowell. (Private Collection.)

Can you imagine putting this preening Pintail Drake in your hunting rig? Though never used, this oval-stamped working decoy is Elmer Crowell at his best. The long sprig, realistic feather painting, and the graceful head make this a masterpiece. (Private Collection).

Red-Breasted Merganser Drake by Cleon Crowell. The owner had a hen made by Elmer and needed a drake to finish out the pair. Elmer had died so Cleon filled the order. As you can see, he's an excellent carver in his own right. (Collection of A.B. Rose)

Elmer Crowell Mallard Drake 1/2 size. (Collection of A.B. Rose).

3 Burr Family Black Bellied Plovers. Rare feeding position with dropped tail carving. In near mint condition, these shorebirds are among the finest folk art extant Hingham, Mass. Circa 1910. (Collection J. Delph).

Rare Crowell Wood Duck Drake decorative decoy. (Collection of Steve Tyng).

Massachusetts Plover-a wonderful piece of American folk art. (Collection of Steve Miller).

Oversized Nantucket Yellowlegs almost 12'' in length. It has 3 piece hollow construction with a visible horizontal seam. The very deep tail separation, tack eyes, and original bill and paint enhance its simple lines. (Collection of Steve Miller).

Very early Massachusetts Yellowlegs with wing and tail carving. (Collection of Steve Miller).

Very unusual Massachusetts Root head. (Collection of Steve Miller).

Magnificent Elmer Crowell Preening Black Duck. Unusual chip carving on body. (Private Collection).

Elmer Crowell Red-Breasted Merganser Drake. Note the detail on the saw-bill. (Collection of Steve Tyng).

An example of Crowell's highest grade of decoy. The Redhead Drake has a turned head and raised wing tip carving. (Private Collection).

Elmer Crowell Red-Breasted Mergansers. The white paint along the bottom is original, although the reason for it is not certain. It's also been found on other species he carved. (Collection of Joe Tonelli).

Elmer Crowell Mallard Drake. (Collection of John and Betty Jean Mulak).

Canada Goose carved by A.E. Crowell. (Collection of Robert L. Dwyer).

←   Massachusetts Canada goose with canvas over wire frame construction. Exceptionally carved wooden head. (Collection of Steve Miller).

←   Massachusetts Red-breasted Merganser drake by unknown maker. (Collection of John Delph).

A trio of Massachusetts shore birds with 3 piece laminated construction. (Collection of Steve Miller).

Red-breasted Merganser Drake by A.E. Crowell. (Oval brand). Super paint-mint condition decoy. (Collection of George Thompson).

Red-breasted Merganser Drakes by A. Elmer Crowell, East Harwich, Mass. Circa 1905. From the S. Gilbert Hinsdale Rig, Buzzards Bay, Mattapossett, Mass. (Left, collection of Alan G. Haid. Right, collection of Robert L. Dwyer).

Extremely rare Crowell Wood Duck Drake hunting decoy. It has an oval brand (after 1915) and a carved crest. (Collection of Tony Waring).

The wood duck is a working decoy and extremely rare. The trio of Black-bellied Plovers were made in 1913 by Crowell. They were found washed up on shore after the 1938 hurricane. These must be about the best decoys by any carver known. (Collection of Tony Waring).

Elmer Crowell Pintail Drake with raised carved wingtips and classic sprig tail. Circa 1900. (Private Collection).

Red-breasted Merganser Drake by Elmer Crowell. (Private Collection).

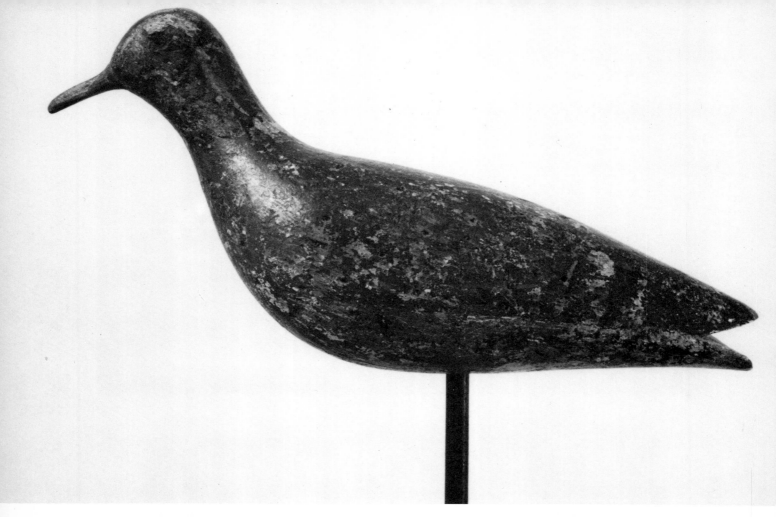

Plover attributed to John Mayhew. Oak Bluff, Marthas Vineyard. This old shorebird has experienced some very demanding service .

3 Massachusetts Yellowlegs "flatties."(Collection of Bill LaPointe).

Battle-scarred Nantucket Plover with split-tail and tack eyes. (Collection of Steve Miller).

Very early unknown Massachusetts willett. Note eyelet under bottom of tail for stringing shorebirds to carry. (Collection of Steve Miller).

Unknown Golden Plover. Very fine paint and split tail make this bird a classic. (Private Collection).

A. Elmer Crowell Blue Bill Hen. The lowest grade made by Crowell but still great by any standards. (Shelburne Museum).

Early Crowell Red-head Drake with raised crossed-wing tips and notched carving on the tail. Pre-stamp Crowell. (Shelburne Museum).

Red-head Drake by A.E. Crowell. Lacks the fine carving detail of the one above, but masterful painting makes this outstanding. (Shelburne Museum).

Martha's Vineyard Merganser with carved eyes, serated crest, and traces of original paint. (Collection of Steve Miller).

Red-breasted Merganser drake. (Collection of Bob Dwyer). Maker unknown.

Unknown Massachusetts American Merganser in original paint. (Collection of Steve Miller).

Mallard Hen by A.E. Crowell. His expertise with a paint brush is evident. (Collection of George Thompson).

←   Crowell Lowhead Goldeneye Drake with carved wing tips. The bottom board is original, with the oval Crowell brand present. The decoy is not hollow and the reason for putting on the board is not known. (Private Collection).

←   Elmer Crowell Red-Breasted Hen Merganser with swimming head position. (Collection of John & Betty Jean Mulak).

Elmer Crowell Green-Wing Teal Drake, probably a decorative. (Collection of Steve Tynge).

Unknown Massachusetts Golden Plover. The unusual bill is doweled into the head. Carved thighs and the split tail are distinctive features. (Private Collection.)

Massachusetts Golden Plover. (Collection of Donald Scothorne).

JOSEPH WHITING LINCOLN

(1859-1938) ACCORD (HINGHAM), MASSACHUSETTS

One word commonly used to describe Joseph Lincoln's decoys is simplicity - simplicity of paint and form. he didn't rely on intricate head and wing carving or elaborate feather painting, although Lincoln was a masterful carver and painter. His simple decoys reflected a simple lifestyle.

Born and raised in Accord, Massachusetts, (now part of Hingham) Lincoln worked as a shoemaker, clock repairer, upholsterer, and decoy maker during his lifetime. Excellent hunting was readily available at Accord Pond, where he spent his early years observing waterfowl in an ideal habitat. He started carving decoys in his teens when he needed a rig of his own and couldn't afford to buy them. Lucky for today's collectors!

Lincoln lived across the street from Accord Pond and carved his stools in a small workshop in back of his house. He gathered dead wood from the cypress swamp in the dead of winter. This cedar was used to make the bodies and seasoned sugar pine for the heads. Unfortunately, the cedar bodies have split over the years, even on many in excellent condition otherwise. This indicates a weakness in the wood he used rather than hard use. All his ducks were painted outside under the trees, regardless of the season. Only hand tools such as an axe, drawknife, and a hatchet were ever used; he didn't think power tools gave the right control.

A quiet man, Joseph Lincoln was a batchelor until the age of 60, when he married Mary, 25 years his junior. He loved flowers and raised prize-winning dahlias. A friend from Hingham remembers driving Lincoln to flower shows and competitions because he didn't drive a car, only rode a bicycle. The 1945 pictures of the Accord Gun Club came from the Whiting family, Lincoln's relatives. They recalled his love of hunting and his excellent shooting ability. He carved into his 70's and was listed in the 1930 Hingham phone directory as:

Joseph Lincoln Age 70 Decoy maker

A complete line of decoys was offered for sale: Black Ducks, Canada Geese, Scoters, Old Squaws, Goldeneyes, and Mergansers, with the first 3 being the most common. Many special orders of other species were carved and found their way onto collector's shelves.

Lincoln's slat geese or "loomers" were used to attract the attention of high-flying flocks. Because they were heavy and awkward to handle, they remained out on the water the entire hunting season. Three slat geese were attached to a triangular base, one in each corner, then anchored in place. While the horizontal slats formed a rather crude body, the head was skillfully carved. More for the maker's satisfaction than the geese he was luring into range.

His canvas and wooden geese were made in several head positions and are highly prized today. The "hissing" goose is a remarkable example of Lincoln's expertise. The graceful neck and the typical squiggled paint pattern found on his geese and brant are exceptional. Lincoln is also known for his miniature duck carvings, small scale replicas of his working ducks. Many different species are found.

Joe Lincoln certainly ranks as one of the premier New England carvers, and many put him in the top 10 in the country. We heartily agree.

Joseph Lincoln at work on some Black Ducks. This was used in a newspaper article in 1927.

Original postcard advertisement. Note that old decoys were repaired and repainted by Lincoln.

J. W. LINCOLN ❧ WOOD AND CANVAS DECOY OF ALL KINDS

DECOYS MADE FROM ANY MODEL. .. .. ❧ ACCORD, MASS
OLD DECOYS REPAIRED AND PAINTED

Goldeneye Drake and Hen by Joseph Lincoln with typical paint style.   (Shelburne Museum).

Lincoln Old Squaw Hen-a fitting mate.   (Shelburne Museum).

Old Squaws, known for their endless squawking, are easily decoyed; thus, few were carved.   The drake by Joe Lincoln, is a master-piece. Simple yet striking!   (Shelburne Museum).

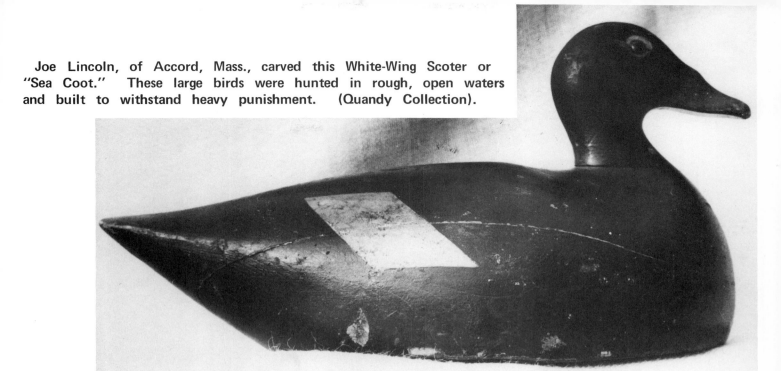

Joe Lincoln, of Accord, Mass., carved this White-Wing Scoter or "Sea Coot." These large birds were hunted in rough, open waters and built to withstand heavy punishment. (Quandy Collection).

Joseph Lincoln Black Duck. (Collection of Tom Winstel).

Exceedingly rare Joe Lincoln American Merganser Hen. (Quandy Collection).

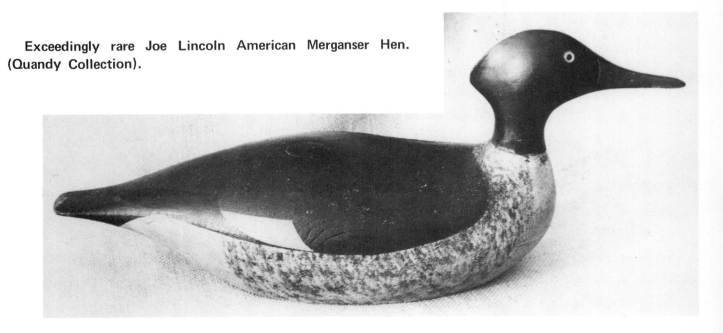

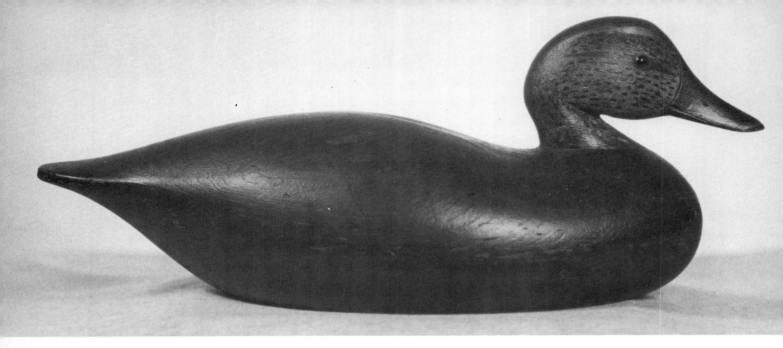

Late period Lincoln Black Duck. The beautifully carved and painted head compliments the plain body. (Collection of George Thompson).

Atlantic Brant by Joeseph W. Lincoln, Accord, Mass. Circa 1925. (Collection of Alan G. Haid).

One of Joe Lincoln's later period Black Ducks. (Private Collection).

Joe Lincoln Brant.   (Quandy Collection).

Joseph Lincoln American Merganser Hen.   (Collection of Tom Winstel).

Large-body Joe Lincoln goose in original though worn paint.   (Collection of Steve Tyng).

Joseph Lincoln American Brant in pristine condition. Brant were heavily hunted in the Atlantic Flyway prior to the early 1930's. Eel-grass, their main source of food, disappeared around 1932 and their numbers steadily declined. They were protected by the Federal Government until their numbers were restored.

Market gunners slaughtered them in great numbers because they brought good money. Hunters found them good sport because of their wariness.

Brant generally would decoy only to stools of their own species. (Collection of George Thompson).

Joseph Lincoln Canada Goose.   (Private Collection).

Slat goose by Joseph Lincoln.   (Private Collection).

This Lincoln Canada Goose has never seen the water, yet traveled from Mass. To New York. Joe Lincoln gave it to a local game warden, Chateau, who in turn gave it to Bob Clifford, a game warden on Cape Cod. Each enjoyed the gift so much, it resided on the mantle, not in the boat house. (Collection of George Thompson).

Battle-scarred Lincoln Goose retains most of its original paint. (Collection of A.B. Rose).

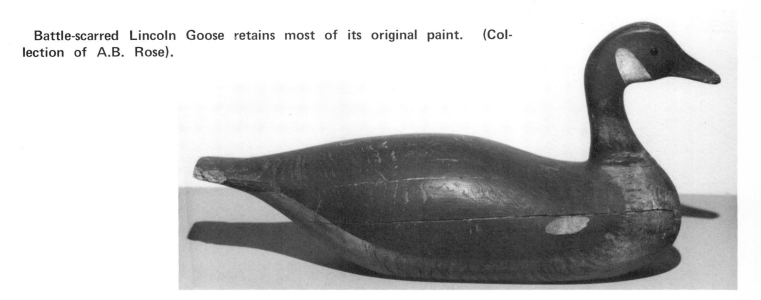

Joseph Lincoln Weathervane. It was made by Lincoln for a friend of his. (Private Collection).

These Lincoln Canada Geese in the swimming position are ½ actual size. On the bottom is his brand. Joe Lincoln, Accord, Mass. (Shelburne Museum).

Massachusetts Split-tail Willet. Similar to shorebird decoys attributed to Joe Lincoln. (Collection of Steve Miller).

Lincoln "Self-Bailing" White-Winged Scoter. This decoy is hollow with a large opening under the tail. They were used in rough water, and the opening allowed the water to run out. Thus, it rode in the water more smoothly. (Shelburne Museum).

Joe Lincoln's hallmark-utter simplicity-is exemplified in this Old Squaw Hen. (Collection of George Thompson).

Very rare Lincoln Bufflehead Drake. Few carvers made Bufflehead decoys because their small size made them unpopular with market hunters. They were hard to hit and brought little money at market, so few blocks are found. (Shelburne Museum).

A. ELMER CROWELL (1862-1952)

EAST HARWICH, MASSACHUSETTS

Live decoys, night shooting, baiting with corn, gunning for market, shorebird hunting-all these were the lifeblood of hunting as Elmer Crowell grew up. Today we look back at the senseless slaughter with indignation, yet according to the sporting laws of their time, they did no wrong, they felt no guilt. At the age of 84, Elmer reminisced about the "good old days" before all the laws and regulations. He was truly a man who loved to hunt.

His first serious hunting began at twelve, after he received a 12 gauge shotgun from his father. By 14, Crowell was using live decoys and 9 wooden blocks he had carved himself. Ninety-five Blackducks plus a few more ducks were listed in his first hunting record book. Not a bad start.

He became proficient at handling live duck and decoys, with ingenious methods for using them. He spent many years as a decoy handler, guide, and market gunner until he went to work running a gunning camp for Dr. Phillips of Beverly, Massachusetts, from 1898-1908.

It wasn't until after this time that Crowell gave up hunting and turned to carving wooden duck decoys. Ornamental birds made in series of 25 were added to his repertoire: 25 shorebirds, 25 song birds, and 25 ducks.

He returned to hunting briefly around 1918 when his son, Cleon, returned from the war. After several years, the laws became so restrictive that Elmer Crowell put his gun away forever.

Decoy carving occupied his time until 1944, when rheumatism forced him to retire after nearly 40 years of carving. He died in 1952 at the age of 90, a master of his craft.

Crowell used split swamp cedar for the solid bodies and pine for the heads. Over the years some of the bodies have checked and split, about the only criticism voiced about Crowell's decoys. Though he had no

formal art training, Crowell had enormous artistic talent as carver and painter. What he could do with housepaint is astounding! The subtle feathering and colorations he achieved were phenomonal. His artist's medium was wood, not canvas.

Elmer Crowell sold thre styles or grades of decoys.

Early Style

This featured cuts on the flat portion of the tail, carved primary feathers and carved crossed wing tips. There usually was rasping on the breast and the back of the head. They were not branded and were made prior to 1915. Collectors feel these are his best decoys.

Intermediate Style

In 1915, Crowell started branding decoys with an oval brand. The decoys are more streamlined and carving detail is eliminated except for the notches on the top of the tail. The primary feathers are painted rather than carved.

Later Style

A rectangular brand was used on his later birds but no exact date is known. There was no carving on these ducks other than the rasping and the feather were indicated with paint. This is the grade sold in Iver Johnson's store in Boston, beautiful yet functional.

Shorebirds by Crowell are equally as collectible as his duck and goose decoys. These too, came in varying degrees of quality and detail. The turned head Black-Bellied Plovers and the feeder found on the cover were imitations of shorebirds in natural positions. Other working shorebirds also impart this feeling of naturalness and spontaneity.

A. Elmer Crowell, an artist in every sense of the word, created decoys any collector would proudly display.

Elmer Crowell Red-Breasted Merganser Hen after many seasons of hard use. (Collection of A.B. Rose).

Crowell Goldeneye Drake, a well-used working decoy.

The original sign that hung outside his shop. (Collection of A.B. Rose).

Ruddy Turnstone by A.E. Crowell. (Collection of Stever Miller).

Crowell Black Duck-circa 1911. (Quandy Collection).

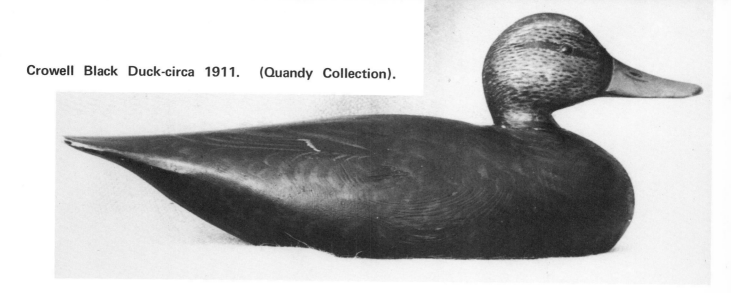

Elmer Crowell Lowhead Black Duck, pre-stamp decoy. (Quandy Collection).

Elmer Crowell Tack-Eye working decoys. Yellowlegs on the left and Golden Plover on the right. (Collection of Steve Tyng).

A pristine Elmer Crowell Dowitcher found in Chatham, Massachusetts. (Collection of Steve Miller).

Elmer Crowell Redhead Drake-oval brand. (Quandy Collection).

Rare Crowell Canvas Back Drake. The raised carved tail feathers and the carving on the sides make this an exceptional one indeed. (Collection of Steve Tyng).

Elmer Crowell Golden Plover working decoy. (Quandy Collection).

Stamp from Iver Johnson Sporting Goods Store in Boston. Black Duck is Supreme grade sold in the store. (Private Collection).

Elmer Crowell Canada Goose.   (Collection of Tom Winstel).

Pintail Hen and Blackduck by A.Elmer Crowell, East Harwich, Mass. Circa 1925. From the Toussiant Shooting Club, Port Clinton, Ohio. Mr. Hoover, of the Vacuum Cleaner fortune, bought a large rig of Mallards, Blacks, Widgeons and Pintails from Elmer during a trip to Boston in 1925. Decoys bear "Hoover" and Crowell oval stamp on the bottom. (Collection of Alan G. Haid.)

Oval Brand on Crowell Black Duck used in Harwich, Massachusetts. (3-1/8" x 1-7/8"). He started using this brand after 1915. The turned head and oversized body enhance this later example of Crowell's work. The crossed wing feathers are painted and breast and head rasping is evident. (Collection of Ned Covington).

148

Rare Crowell Flattie Yellowlegs, used as a working decoy. Flatties were lighter to carry than a rig of full-bodied shorebirds. (Collection of John Mulak).

Elmer Crowell Lowhead Whistler Hen-oval brand. (Quandy Collection)

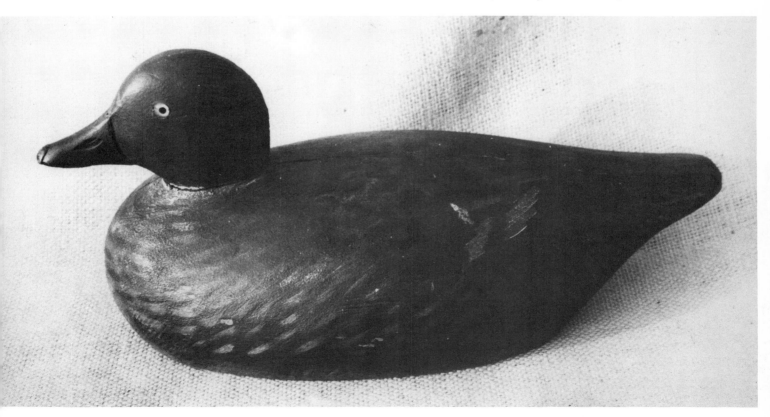

This Preening Black Duck by Elmer Crowell must be one of the top 10 duck decoys in the country. The raised wing, carved separately, is attached by wooden dowels. The preening neck and head seem to be in suspended animation. (Shelburne Museum).

Elmer Crowell Pintail Drake. Found on Long Island and Branded Hazelton. (Quandy Collection).

Elmer Crowell Redhead Hen. Note the rasping on the head and breast and the notched tail carving.

Elmer Crowell Canada Goose-oval brand. (Quandy Collection).

Elmer Crowell Blue Bill Drake. (Quandy Collection).

Elmer Crowell Black Duck-circa 1930. (Quandy Collection).

Oval Stamp-Elmer Crowell Pintail Hen. From the Hazelton Rig, Long Island, N.Y. (Quandy Collection).

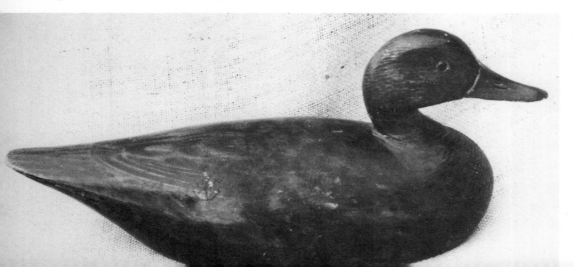

Pre-1900 Elmer Crowell Yellowlegs in mint condition. (Collection of Steve Miller).

Oval stamp (pre-1918) Elmer Crowell Pintail drake with notched tail carving. (Collection of Steve Miller).

Ben Smith Red-Breasted Merganser hen. Forward head position. Hollow. Painted eyes. Worn evidence of crest. Typical weight found on Smith round bottom decoys. (Private Collection).

Bibliography

Carter, Winthrop. *George Boyd The Shorebird Decoy. An American Folk Art.* Tenant House Press, 1978.

Cheever, Bryon. *North American Decoys Magazine.* Hillcrest Publications, 1971-1979.

Colio, Quintina. *American Decoys.* Science Press, 1972.

Earnest, Adele. *The Art of the Decoy.* Clarkson N. Potter, 1965. Reissued Bramhall House.

Mackey, William. *American Bird Decoys.* Dutton, 1965. Reissued, Schiffer Publishing Limited, 1979.

Murphy, Stanley. *Martha's Vineyard Decoys.* David Godine, Publisher, Boston, 1978.

Sorenson, Harold D. *Decoy Collector's Guide.* Harold Sorenson, Publisher 1963-1979.

Starr, George Ross Jr. *Decoys of the Atlantic Flyway,* Winchester Press, 1974.

Webster, David and Kehoe, William. *Decoys at Shelburne Museum.* Shelburne Museum, 1961, 1971.

Lincoln Black Duck (Shelburne Museum)

Index

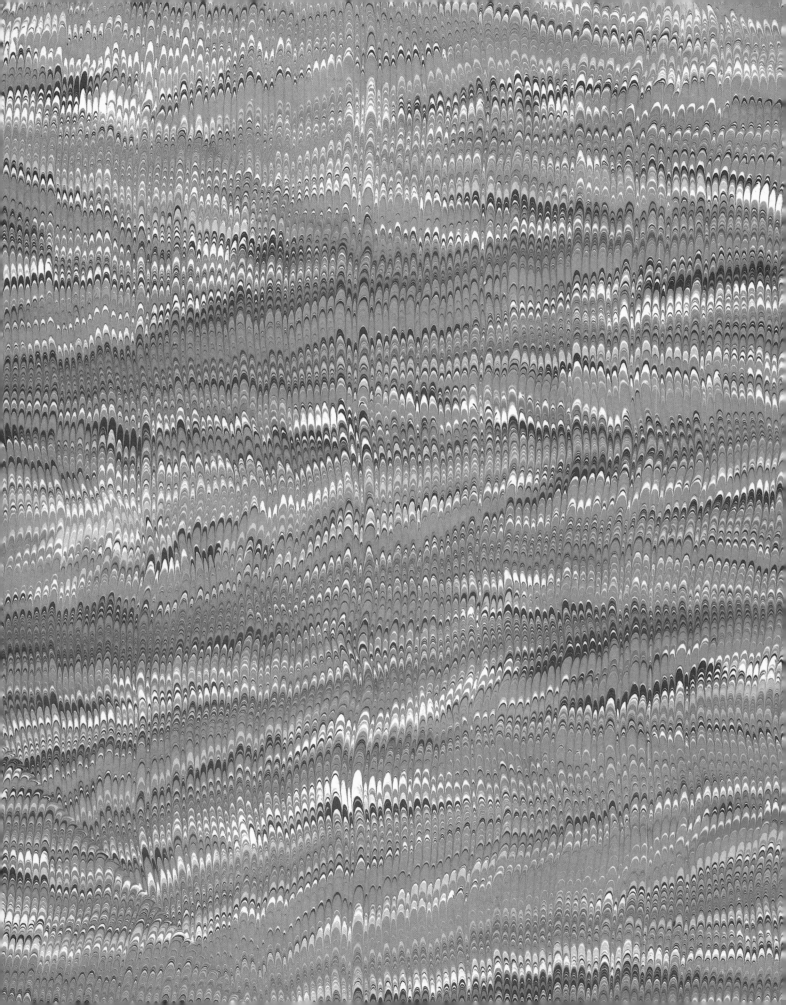